LEARNING ABOUT
Plants

Catherine Veitch

Raintree

Chicago, Illinois

The author would like to dedicate this book to her mother, Jacqueline Veitch, who inspired her with a love of nature.

Edited by Dan Nunn, Rebecca Rissman, and Sian Smith
Designed by Joanna Hinton-Malivoire
Picture research by Mica Brancic
Production by Sophia Argyris
Originated by Capstone Global Library Ltd
Printed in the United States of America in
North Mankato, MN. 012014 007974RP

Library of Congress Cataloging-in-Publication Data
Veitch, Catherine.
  Learning about plants / Catherine Veitch.—1st ed.
      p. cm.—(The natural world)
  Includes bibliographical references and index.
ISBN 978-1-4109-5401-5 (hb)
ISBN 978-1-4109-5406-0 (pb)
1. Plants—Juvenile literature. I. Title. II. Series: Natural world (Chicago, Ill.)
QK49.V38 2013
580—dc23   2012049392

Acknowledgments

The author and publisher are grateful to the following for permission to reproduce copyright material: Alamy: Imagebroker.net, 4 (top inset), 24; Science Source: Dr Jeremy Burgess, 4 (bottom inset), 23; Shutterstock: a9photo, back cover, 20, Anest, 16 (inset), Antonio Abrignani, 12 (inset), 23, aodaodaodaod, 13, Chepko Danil Vitalevich, 24 (top), Dave Head, 5, 24, de2marco, 10 (inset), 22, ER_09, 16, Gabriela Insuratelu, 18, Galyna Andrushko, 6, Igor Normann, 4, 22, Katharina Wittfeld, 19, 24, LianeM, cover, Martin Fowler, 12, 23, Maxim Blinkov, 11, Neirfy, 8, 22, Panitchon, 7, saiva_l, 17, Serg64, 14, 22, Sergey Galushko, 15, 23, szabozoltan, 9, 23, Timolina, 10, yuriy kulik, 21.

We would like to thank Michael Bright for his invaluable help in the preparation of this book.

Every effort has been made to contact copyright holders of any material reproduced in this book. Any omissions will be rectified in subsequent printings if notice is given to the publisher.

Contents

Blackberry

Bluebell

Bulrush

Cosmos

Freesia

Honesty

Hyacinth

Ivy

Orchid

Pitcher Plant

13

Poppy

Rose

Strawberry

Sweet Pea

Teasel

18

Tomato

Venus Flytrap

20

Water Lily

Picture Glossary

bud part of a plant that grows into a new leaf or a flower

bulb some plants grow out of bulbs in the ground. Bulbs are like food stores. Food in the bulb helps a plant grow.

flower part of a plant that makes seeds. The smells flowers make and their colors help attract insects.

fruit fruits hold seeds. Plants make fruit so that animals will eat the fruit and carry the seeds to new places.

leaf part of a plant. Leaves use sunlight to make food for the plant.

petal one of the colored parts of a flower

pollen powder inside a flower. Pollen has to move from flower to flower or plant to plant for plants to make seeds.

roots part of a plant that holds the plant in the ground. Roots bring water to the plant.

seed pod case that holds seeds and helps keep them safe

seeds plants make seeds. Seeds grow into new plants.

stem part of a plant from which the leaves and flowers grow. Stems hold plants up and carry water to different parts of the plant.

thorn hard, sharp point that sticks out from the stems of some plants. Thorns help stop animals from eating the plant.

vine long, winding stem that creeps along the ground or climbs up things

Notes for Parents and Teachers

- Go on a nature walk with the children. Help them identify different plants and their parts. Children can sketch or photograph what they see.
Use the pictures to create a class book.
- Collect different flowers and leaves. Discuss the different shapes and colors of the flowers and leaves. Press the flowers and add these and the leaves to the class book.
Remind children to always check with an adult that flowers and leaves are safe to collect, and to always wash their hands after handling flowers and leaves.